642

THINGS TO WRITE ABOUT

Young Writer's Edition

BY 826 VALENCIA

INTRODUCTION BY MIRANDA TSANG

chronicle books · san francisco

CONTRIBUTORS
••••••••••••

Alexis Sattler
Amanda Meth
Austin Hoffmann
Byron Weiss
Carol Dorf
Carrie Clements
Colin Winnette
Cristina Marie
Dawna Kemper
Diane Wright
Doreen Finn
Emilie Coulson
Emmanuelle Joyeux
Ian Anderson
Ian Evans
Iris Lerch
Isaac Fitzgerald
Janice Green
Jeni Paltiel
Jennifer Larson

Jessica Berrios
Joe Lash
Joey Bien-Kahn
Jon Schleuning
Karen Lewis
Karen Wagstaffe
Katrina Plam
Linda Antonioli
Lindsey Plait Jones
Marie Payment
Marissa Carter
Marlene Cullen
Mildred Dzib
Miranda Tsang
Molly Parent
Nancy Ware
Naoki O'Bryan
Natalie Warner
Nínive Calegari
Olivia White Lopez
Paris Kim
Parissa Ebrahimzadeh

Paul Cartier
Rachel Khong
Randy Hyde
Ronaldo Rodriguez
Ryan Lewis
Sam Larson
Sam Riley
Sean Tracy
Shannon David
Shannon Weber
Sheila Doucet
Silvi Alcivar
Sofia Marquez
Sondra Hall
Stephen Sparks
Tara Fatemi
Taylor Yeomans
Tim R
Tommy Mike
Yvonne Lerch
Zola Rosenfeld

Library of Congress Cataloging-in-Publication Data available.

ISBN 978-1-4521-2784-2

Manufactured in China.

Design by Eloise Leigh.

10 9 8 7 6

Chronicle Books LLC
680 Second Street
San Francisco, CA 94107

Chronicle Books — we see things differently.
Become part of our community at www.chroniclekids.com.

AT 826 VALENCIA, we believe that kids can be authors. Elementary-school students visit 826, write an entire book, and take it home in just two hours. Our middle-school students interview actors, boxers, and local politicians as they write the scoops for their school newspapers and lifestyle magazines (you heard it here first, lifestyle magazines for middle-school students!). And we work with high-school students every year to coach them through drafting, editing, and producing a collection of writing that is sold at stores around the city and available worldwide. Young people have important and interesting things to say, and 826 helps students put their great ideas down in writing.

Now that you own this book, we are claiming you as an honorary 826 student — consider this the course to spark your creativity and practice your writing skills using prompts, the way 826 Valencia students do every day. You can follow this book page by page, or you can fling it open, point at a prompt, and write furiously until you've conquered every square inch of blank space. Our best advice for you is to use this book in whatever way is best for you. Don't worry if you get stuck on a prompt — skip it and work on another one. You might fall in love with something you write for that prompt on page ten and finish a whole novel on that topic!

Whenever you work your way to the end of this book, write your own About the Author (that's you), and give your writing advance praise. (Calvin's work reminds me of a young Hemingway! Sofia's story is well-written and sophisticated!) Copy and share your work with friends, make a little book of your writing, or create a blog (with your parents' permission, of course) and share it with family and friends far and wide, and congrats, you're an author!

When we put together this book for students around the world, we consulted kid brains, writer brains, pirate brains, and tutor brains to bring you writing prompts that we hope will spark excitement and lots and lots of writing.

Now flip to another page of this book and start writing. What are you waiting for?

MIRANDA TSANG
Communications Manager, 826 Valencia

You're enjoying making sand castles at the beach, when the ocean waves wash up a message in a bottle. You pull out the message: What does it say?

An old couple stops you in the street and says you'd be perfect for the job . . .

The entire neighborhood is beige and gray, but at the end of the street sits a bright blue house. Who lives there?

The king shows up on your doorstep . . .

Write a story that includes a streetlight, a bear, and a kid
with a jar of honey.

....

....

....

....

....

....

....

....

....

....

....

....

....

....

....

....

....

Astronauts land on a distant planet. As soon as they open the shuttle door,
they see the most amazing sight. Write about the adventures the astronauts
have as they explore the new planet.

....

....

....

....

....

....

....

....

....

....

....

....

....

....

....

....

....

A group of students are hiking, when they come across a nest with
golden eggs. At that moment, one of the eggs hatches.

....

....

....

....

....

....

You're in the middle of a coffee shop, and time grinds to a
halt. Describe the scene.

....

....

....

....

....

....

You find the end of the rainbow . . .

....

....

....

....

....

....

Write about something you hate to love.

....

....

....

....

....

....

....

....

One morning Jessica wakes up and realizes she is magnetic.

....

....

....

....

....

....

....

....

Jeff has just scored the winning goal in the football championship. He is a hero, and he is being carried on the shoulders of his teammates. You are the reporter who gets to interview Jeff.

....

....

....

....

....

....

....

....

....

....

....

....

....

....

....

....

....

....

Describe a situation where you feel very uncomfortable.

....

....

....

....

....

....

....

....

All the glass in the world has disappeared.

....

....

....

....

....

....

....

....

You meet a girl who, when she closes her eyes, can see the entire universe. Tell us about this girl.

The cardboard box took up half of the room . . .

There were pancakes everywhere.

You realize your crush is following you home. What do you do?

You find out your neighbor's brick house is actually made of painted books.
Which one do you want to read, and what happens when you take it?

....

....

....

....

....

....

....

....

....

....

....

....

....

....

....

....

....

....

You watch an old movie and realize it's about you.

....

....

....

....

....

....

....

....

....

....

....

....

....

....

....

....

....

Describe a dream you remember.

....

....

....

....

....

....

....

....

Describe trying to remember a dream.

....

....

....

....

....

....

....

....

A light in your backyard gets brighter and brighter, until . . .
Flash! Flash! Flash! What causes these flashes? Where are you, and
how do they affect you?

....

....

....

....

....

....

....

....

What does your dog do when you're away? Does it go on adventures or
guard the house? If it sleeps, what does it dream about?

....

....

....

....

....

....

....

....

He dodged the fish and
swam fast . . .

List five names that would be
perfect for an evil villain.

You see a picture of yourself
in a newspaper. It says
you have disappeared.
What is going on?

Two people get stuck on a roller
coaster ride together.
What do they talk about?

Congratulations! You're a teacher now and can teach any class you want. It can be normal (grammar) or new (advanced magic theory). What would students do in class? What would the homework be? What would students be graded on?

....

....

....

....

....

....

....

....

....

....

....

....

....

....

....

....

Write a guidebook about a place you've been to only in stories. It could
be a place that your parents talk about all the time or the setting of
your favorite book.

....

....

....

....

....

....

....

....

....

....

....

....

....

....

....

....

....

....

....

When was the first time you left your hometown? Where did you go,
and with whom? What was the same, and what was different? Were you
nervous, even just a little bit?

....

....

....

....

....

....

....

....

Congratulations! You've won a trip to Mars. The rocket leaves in a few
days; what will you pack? Please keep in mind it might be a long time
before you go back home.

....

....

....

....

....

....

....

....

What's something that you can do better than anyone else you know?
Making pancakes? Algebra? Telling stories set on the moon? Write a
how-to guide about your area of expertise.

....

....

....

....

....

....

....

....

....

....

....

....

....

....

....

....

....

....

What's your favorite word? What makes it special? Is it the sounds,
the meaning, the way the letters look on the page?

....

....

....

....

....

....

Does your house have feelings? Is it grumpy, happy, or somewhere in
between? How old is it? If it could tell a story, what would it tell?

....

....

....

....

....

....

What's your favorite meal? Who cooks it best? What does the meal
remind you of?

....

....

....

....

....

....

Write a story about a penguin that rhymes (so good you can tell it a thousand times!).

....

....

....

....

....

....

....

....

....

What color was the sky on your first day of school? What were you wearing? Did you meet any friends? Did you learn anything new?

....

....

....

....

....

....

....

....

Your parents go out of town
for the weekend and you have
the house to yourself.
What happens?

A girl is sitting on a park bench
looking around for somebody.
Whom is she waiting for?

Write a witch's spell.

Write a poem about a bear.

Create a place exactly like Earth but with one big difference.

Pick a famous historical figure and write a dialogue between that person and their parents.

....

....

....

....

....

....

A short man walks into the grocery store wearing a
strange hat. Describe him and what happens.

....

....

....

....

....

....

Describe the perfect bedroom. How would your room look
if you could do anything you wanted to it?

....

....

....

....

....

....

Think of a bad habit, and write a scene where the main character can't
stop doing it.

....

....

....

....

....

....

....

....

Write the lyrics to a song about summer.

....

....

....

....

....

....

....

....

Choose a villain from one of your favorite stories. Write about the world
the way they see it. Give that person a chance to explain their actions.

....

....

....

....

....

....

....

....

....

....

....

....

....

....

....

....

....

....

The most embarrassing thing you can think of has just happened
to somebody. They leave the room crying. What happens next?

....

....

....

....

....

....

....

....

What would a good hideout be like?

....

....

....

....

....

....

....

....

Write the tale of a knight who comes to rescue a princess who is trapped
in a tower and guarded by a dragon, but tell the story from the dragon's
perspective. Or maybe the princess has come to save the dragon, who is
trapped in a tower guarded by the knight. Or the dragon has come to rescue
the knight who is trapped in a tower guarded by the princess. Or maybe they
all just go out for brunch. It's your adventure!

A boy quickly sticks something in his pocket. What is it and why?

If you could meet one scary character, whom would you meet?

Tell somebody's entire life story in one sentence.

If you could shrink until you were the size of a mouse, where would you go?

Somebody packs a suitcase in a hurry. Why?

....

....

....

....

....

....

What is the real story behind your favorite song?

....

....

....

....

....

....

Invent a new type of breakfast food.

....

....

....

....

....

....

Describe the perfect world. What does it look like?
What kind of people would live there?

....

....

....

....

....

....

....

....

....

....

....

....

....

....

....

....

....

....

A journalist has just discovered something big. What's the scoop?

....

....

....

....

....

....

....

....

Think of the worst fight you ever had and write it from the other person's perspective.

....

....

....

....

....

....

....

....

Come up with a new word. What does it mean?

....

....

....

....

....

....

What does the food in your refrigerator do when you close the door?

....

....

....

....

....

....

What would you do if you were stuck in a bathroom?

....

....

....

....

....

....

A bird has been following you everywhere you go for a week. Why is it
following you? Whom does it work for?

....

....

....

....

....

....

For one day you can snap your fingers and live that day as any historical
figure. Who will you choose? King Tut? Helen Keller? Genghis Khan?

....

....

....

....

....

....

A dog as big as a house shows up in your neighborhood. He wants to play.

....

....

....

....

....

....

You are a fortune-teller. Predict what will happen in your best friend's future.

....

....

....

....

....

....

....

....

What happens on a superhero's day off?

....

....

....

....

....

....

....

....

Scientists have found a new island, and you have been asked to develop this new territory. What does the island look like? Who lives here? What are the rules/laws of this new place, and what language will its residents speak?

....

....

....

....

....

....

....

....

....

....

....

....

....

....

....

....

If you had to make a robot, what would it do? How would it help you?

....

....

....

....

....

....

....

....

You're reading your favorite picture book, when suddenly the pictures come to life. Who are these characters? What are they like in real life? Do you keep this a secret?

....

....

....

....

....

....

....

....

What would you do if your parents forgot to pick you up after school?

What would you do if you had to live in a cave?

You wake up one morning unable to talk or write. How will you communicate to those around you?

You're playing a game by yourself, when a ghost starts playing with you.

You are given the ability to solve just one of the world's biggest problems.
Which do you choose? How would solving this problem change the person you are?
Who exactly is affected by this solution? Would everyone agree with your decision?

....

....

....

....

....

....

....

....

....

....

....

....

....

....

....

....

....

What if there were no natural disasters in the world?
What would the earth look like?

....

....

....

....

....

....

You're sitting at a café, and when you get up to get a refill, you notice
someone has dropped a note on your seat. What does the note say? Who left it?

....

....

....

....

....

....

If you were in the ocean and you saw something that was
about to blow up, what would you do?

....

....

....

....

....

....

You fall asleep in math class and have a nightmare. What happens? Do you make a sudden movement in your chair? Do people notice? Are you drooling?

....

....

....

....

....

....

....

....

....

....

....

....

....

....

....

....

....

Become the ocean and write it out: What kind of ocean are you? Filled with jellyfish or merpeople? Would you be dark and thunderous or warm and calm? Get detailed. Get imaginative.

....

....

....

....

....

....

....

....

....

....

....

....

....

....

....

....

....

....

Think of a time when you made a decision that you later regretted. Was it something that changed your life or someone's close to you? How would your life have changed if you did things differently? How would it be the same?

....

....

....

....

....

....

....

....

You have a dream in which you have to redesign the flag with a modern and edgy look. When you do, people don't like it and are angry. They chase you. What are they waving?

....

....

....

....

....

....

....

....

What would you do if you were stuck in a volcano?

....

....

....

....

....

....

Imagine you're inside a cocoon before it opens. What do you
see? What are the colors and shapes that fill the walls?

....

....

....

....

....

....

What would life be like if you woke up and you were a dog? Would
you eat dog food or people food? Would you chase after cats?

....

....

....

....

....

....

If you were a bug and you were stuck underground for 1,000,000,000,000 years, what would you do until you got out?

A long time ago people did things differently . . .

I hate to tell you this but . . .

Write about what it would be like to hang out on a cloud. Is it rainy? Is it soft? How big is the cloud, and can anyone join you?

Find a photograph and write down everything that happened up until that picture was taken. What's the story behind this one moment? What's going on in the parts of the photo we can't see?

....

....

....

....

....

....

....

....

....

....

....

....

....

....

....

....

....

....

One morning, you find that you can no longer taste foods,
but only their ingredients.

....

....

....

....

....

....

....

....

You are given the opportunity to either go to the moon or stay
on Earth with the power to fly. Which one do you choose?

....

....

....

....

....

....

....

....

One night you're walking home, when you see a meteor rushing
toward Earth. What do you do? Do you warn the people around you?
What if they don't believe you?

....

....

....

....

....

....

....

....

What's the saddest thing you've ever felt? What did it feel
like? How did you overcome this sadness?

....

....

....

....

....

....

....

....

Write a 26-line poem. Start with an "A" word. Each line should start with a different letter from the alphabet, in alphabetical order. The last line should start with a "Z" word.

Write about a time when you did a good deed but couldn't tell anyone about it.
What was it, and why couldn't you tell anyone? Did this secret cause any problems?

....

....

....

....

....

....

What do you have in your pockets? Make up funny reasons for those
things to be there.

....

....

....

....

....

What's it like under the ground? Do insects and bugs live there?
Can you imagine what life would be like if you lived there?

....

....

....

....

....

NASA has just launched a new program that will allow anyone the chance to go into space for free! However, you must go with a complete stranger.

....

....

....

....

....

....

....

....

....

....

....

....

....

....

....

....

....

....

What I don't like about being
a kid is . . .

This morning I woke up and decided
I wanted to go on an adventure,
so I packed my backpack and hit
the open road.

Tomorrow you will be dropped off
at the airport with a suitcase filled
with money. You're told to go anywhere
you want. Where do you go?

Would you rather be a great singer
or a great dancer?

Find an old magazine with photos. Choose two photos of people or animals. These will be your characters. Create dialogue between your two characters. The first one says, "Will you help me? I need . . ."

....

....

....

....

....

....

....

....

Go outdoors. What's the smallest living thing you notice? The largest? Find something that seems out of place. What do you hear? What do you smell? What words come to mind?

....

....

....

....

....

....

....

....

Write everything you know about being human.

....

....

....

....

....

....

....

....

....

....

....

....

....

....

....

....

....

....

Write everything you don't know about being human.

....

....

....

....

....

....

....

....

....

....

....

....

....

....

....

....

....

....

Take a section of today's newspaper. Find at least ten words or phrases that catch your imagination. Write these words down and use them to create a poem. Your poem should start with the words "If only . . ."

....
....
....
....
....
....
....

If you were an insect for a day, what kind would you be? What does your average day look like?

....
....
....
....
....
....
....
....

If you could make a new country by combining any three other countries, which ones would you choose?

Write a poem in the voice of your favorite cartoon character.

On a warm summer evening I went out to play in my backyard, when suddenly I realized something magical was happening. All the plants and animals were . . .

You can see in the dark.

I was kayaking across the ocean, when I realized I had come to a foreign land. Upon reaching the shore, I got out of my kayak and went exploring . . .

....

....

....

....

....

....

....

....

....

....

....

....

....

....

....

....

....

....

It was my first visit from the tooth fairy and I . . .

....

....

....

....

....

....

Look at a map. Use the language on the map to describe how
someone might find you.

....

....

....

....

....

....

Now add pretend places and try giving the streets/rivers/parks new names.
Be sure to describe what transportation your reader will need to find you.
Add landmarks, special trees, animals, or secret pathways.

....

....

....

....

....

....

If you could switch bodies with your mother or father for one day, would you? Who would you be? Would you go to work and be responsible? Or would you act your real age?

....

....

....

....

....

....

....

....

....

....

....

....

....

....

....

....

....

....

....

Describe your grandmother's and/or grandfather's home,
and the best advice they ever gave you.

You have the power to control the weather for one week. Do you make a giant snowstorm that cancels school for the next few days or do you keep the sun shining while class continues?

....

....

....

....

....

....

....

....

You are hiking through the woods, and you find three dinosaur eggs. What do you do?

....

....

....

....

....

....

....

....

Write down what your dog thinks when it goes outside to play.

....

....

....

....

....

....

I decided to build a sand castle, but I didn't have a shovel
or sand, so I . . .

....

....

....

....

....

You get shrunk down for a science experiment, but the scientist
accidentally drops you on the grass in his garden.

....

....

....

....

....

I was there when the pigs flew.

You are riding on the back of an elephant, when suddenly he gallops away. Where does he take you?

You are sailing to the moon with a talking parrot as your copilot. What do the two of you talk about on the journey?

You are the farmer of an artichoke farm that sits on a cliff by the ocean. Describe your day.

You are sailing the seas, when you discover a whale trapped in netting and separated from its pod. You feel the need to help the whale. Describe your journey getting the whale back to its pod.

....

....

....

....

....

....

....

....

You have been shrunk and are wandering around the flower bushes, when you discover a colony of fairies. The fairies are celebrating a special fairy holiday. What is it, and what types of things do the fairies do to celebrate?

....

....

....

....

....

....

....

....

You are searching for artifacts in the middle of the Sahara desert. As you are digging, you begin to uncover bones belonging to an undiscovered dinosaur. Describe the rest of the adventure.

You are walking in the park, when you fall into a hole that leads to an alternate universe. Describe it. What happens to you while you are there?

....

....

....

....

....

....

....

....

....

....

....

....

....

....

....

....

....

....

You are walking around, when you discover a magical workshop. You walk in. The owner claims she can give you wings. Do you let her?

....

....

....

....

....

....

You discover a talking starfish who asks you to show her what life on land is like, but she can't come out of the water for more than five seconds.

....

....

....

....

....

....

You win tickets to the Olympics, and as you're wandering around the events, a group of Olympic volleyball players mistakes you for one of their team members. You've never played volleyball before in your life.

....

....

....

....

....

You decide to become a street performer. Write about one day in your life.

Accountants have kidnapped you and you are now sailing toward the Caribbean. How do you escape?

A magical raccoon with a rainbow tail climbs through your window.

You are eating dinner with your family, when one of the peas on your plate starts whispering to you. What does it say?

What if your pencils and pens could talk, and every one of them had a different personality? Name five of your writing instruments and what their personalities are.

....

....

....

....

....

....

....

....

You wake up one morning and find that you have transformed into a three-toed sloth. When your mother comes in your room to wake you up, she screams. Then she calls animal control. What happens?

....

....

....

....

....

....

....

....

You are running through a field of bright orange flowers, when you trip over
something sticking out of the ground. You dig up this object to discover it
is a diary. Whose diary is it, and what do you discover by reading it?

....

....

....

....

....

....

....

....

....

....

....

....

....

....

....

....

....

....

On your ninth birthday, every birthday wish you ever wished in your whole
life came true, little by little. Tell it like a story.

....

....

....

....

....

....

....

....

....

....

....

....

....

....

....

....

....

....

You are an oyster diver, and you discover a pearl the size of your house. You are sure nobody has ever discovered it before. Do you keep the pearl a secret or tell the world? What do you do next?

....

....

....

....

....

....

....

....

You love to eat Belgian waffles. You cover them in sticky syrup and stuff them in your mouth. Your mother tells you that if you keep eating Belgian waffles for breakfast, lunch, and dinner, you will turn into one. Then one day you do.

....

....

....

....

....

....

....

....

Your parents tell you that you are moving to the Arctic to live in an ice fortress. How do you react, and what happens once you get there?

....

....

....

....

....

....

A cooking show asks you to bake them the biggest cupcake that ever existed. This cupcake needs to be taller than three stories, and wider than a blimp. Describe how you make this cupcake and get it to the TV studio.

....

....

....

....

....

....

You are at the zoo, when all the animals are let out of their cages. When a giant panda has you cornered near the giraffe exhibit you scream, "Stop!" and realize you can communicate with animals. What do you do?

....

....

....

....

....

Someone hands you 100 balloons, and slowly you begin to float upward toward the blue sky. Where do you float off to, and what happens to you along the journey? And when you finally land?

....

....

....

....

....

....

....

....

....

....

....

....

....

....

....

....

....

An owl is hooting outside your window. You notice that he is holding a secret note in his talon. What is the secret note about, and what happens next?

You discover a talking puppy. What do the two of you do for the rest of the day?

You're an ant-size person, and you accidentally fall into an ant hole, deep down into their colony. The ants begin to carry you to their queen.

You get a pair of flying roller skates. Where do you go?

An octopus comes rolling into a gas station in a water tank. He asks you if you can give him a lift to Santa Monica, California. The two of you head out on the road. Five minutes in to the trip, the octopus starts begging you for peanut butter and jelly sandwiches.

....

....

....

....

....

....

....

....

One day you fall asleep on the school bus, and when you wake up you realize you have missed your stop, and the bus is empty. Where are you? How do you get back home? Is there something you need to do before you return home?

....

....

....

....

....

....

....

....

You have a dream involving a box full of erasers and a very, very small
penguin. Fill in the events of that dream. Extra credit: What does having
this dream mean about your real life?

....

....

....

....

....

....

....

....

....

....

....

....

....

....

....

....

....

....

You decide to bring a magical rock to show-and-tell. What happens when the rock starts to shake and rattle at school?

....

....

....

....

....

You find a bunch of kittens in a box on the side of the road. They can't find their mother. What do you do with the kittens, and what do you discover about them?

....

....

....

....

....

A talking cactus tells you his one dream is to ride in a hot air balloon; but he can't move from the ground, and he is afraid he will pop the balloon. How do you help him make his dream come true?

....

....

....

....

....

Write the fantastic story of the origin of April Fools' Day.

....

....

....

....

....

....

....

....

....

....

....

....

....

....

....

....

....

....

Tell the story of how the pot and the tea kettle got into an argument.

Describe your life as a professional snail racer.

Imagine the world if people rode giant grasshoppers instead of driving cars.

Something is missing. What is it? Where has it gone?

One day at the museum, you are staring at the Mona Lisa with signs all
around it that say "Do Not Touch." The famous painting starts talking to
you, and it tells you that it wants to escape its life in the museum.

....

....

....

....

....

....

....

....

Write an argument involving two kids, an apple, and one massive
misunderstanding.

....

....

....

....

....

....

....

....

....

Write a letter to your grandchild about the world you grew up in.

Describe the color red to someone who is color-blind.

....

....

....

....

....

....

....

....

If you could have any pet in the world, what would it be, and how
would you convince your parents to let you keep it?

....

....

....

....

....

....

....

....

Deep in the rain forests of Belize, your mother, who is a healer, discovers
a new plant. She declares that its leaves have an astonishing use. What is
the one strange side effect of this plant's medicine?

....

....

....

....

....

....

....

....

If you could invent any kind of candy, what would it be? Write a little
song to convince people how great your new candy is.

....

....

....

....

....

....

....

....

Write a poem about your favorite food. Make sure to describe
what it tastes like, how it looks, and how it makes you feel.

....

....

....

....

....

....

....

....

....

....

....

....

....

....

....

....

....

Your cat is an evil mastermind and has figured out
how to switch bodies with you.

....

....

....

....

....

....

What's a good song? If you could taste it, smell it,
touch it, and see it, what would it be like?

....

....

....

....

....

Describe the perfect summer.

....

....

....

....

....

....

Phew! Something smells awful! What is it? Why is it so stinky?

You get one magic spell, but you can use it as much as you want. What is it, and what do you do with it?

You are about to go explore the jungle for a week. What three things do you bring, and why?

If you were a superhero, what would your name be, and what would your superpower be?

It's your friend's birthday, and you have an unlimited budget
to plan their party.

....

....

....

....

....

....

....

....

....

....

....

....

....

....

....

....

....

....

A genie grants you three wishes. What do you wish for,
and what's the worst that could happen?

....

....

....

....

....

....

....

....

....

....

....

....

....

....

....

....

....

....

Imagine that two of your favorite characters from two different books, TV shows, or movies meet. Write a conversation between them. How do they speak, and what are they talking about?

....

....

....

....

....

....

....

....

....

A tumbleweed comes blowing by and knocks you onto the set of an old western movie. It's high noon, and the sheriff comes walking toward you with an angry look on his face.

....

....

....

....

....

....

....

....

You are sitting on the beach, reading a book, when a mermaid appears at the water's edge. Her tail turns into legs and she begins to walk away toward the road. What do you do?

....

....

....

....

....

....

....

....

Describe a day as a cheetah.

....

....

....

....

....

....

....

....

You are awoken by a high-pitched
squeal that can be heard throughout
the city. You jump out of bed,
ready for action. What is all the
noise about?

One morning,
everything is different.

You are a cowboy.
Write a poem to your horse.

You meet an old wizard who offers
you the power to fly like a bird or swim
and breathe underwater like a shark.

You are hiking through the forest, when you come upon a tree with a
huge hole in its side. It is the entrance to an underground passage.
You go inside.

....

....

....

....

....

....

....

....

....

....

....

....

....

....

....

....

....

....

You save a puppy from a burning building and become a local hero.
How does your life change because of your newfound celebrity?

....

....

....

....

....

You get onto the bus and see the rest of the passengers pointing at you and
whispering. You are confused and self-conscious until finally a man walks
toward you, taps you on the shoulder, and says, "Excuse me, but . . ."

....

....

....

....

....

Write a story that ends with the line "So it goes in this life on the sea,
where everything's as uncertain as the wind."

....

....

....

....

....

....

Write a short story that begins with the line "Things had been getting stranger and stranger ever since Fred brought that teacup pig home."

....

....

....

....

....

....

....

....

Your best friend tells you that they are a werewolf. They ask you to sleep over during the next full moon to make sure nothing bad happens. Write about your night.

....

....

....

....

....

....

....

....

Write a letter to your hero. Why does that person inspire
you? What do you wish to tell them?

....

....

....

....

....

....

....

....

....

....

....

....

....

....

....

....

....

....

Write an ode to your pet. Make sure to be specific (describe sounds,
smells, tendencies, etc.).

....

....

....

....

....

....

....

....

You are a limo driver for the stars. Write about your most exciting
night on the job.

....

....

....

....

....

....

....

....

You're a toothbrush. Describe someone brushing their teeth from
your point of view.

....

....

....

....

....

You are the king on a chessboard. What is life like? Are you consumed by
your power? Are you frustrated by how little you can move? What do you do
in the hours between games?

....

....

....

....

....

Explain your favorite fruit using exclusively similes and metaphors.
How does it taste? How does it smell? How does eating it make you feel?

....

....

....

....

....

You see the same squirrel ten times in a day. The tenth time, the squirrel squeaks at you and beckons you to follow. You run after it as it leads you to the forest behind your school.

Write a poem from the point of view of a lion at the zoo.

One day you sprout a tail. What do you use it for?

You are the second-fastest human on earth. What is your relationship with the fastest human like?

You are a famous biologist exploring the rain forest and you discover a new species. What do you name the species? What does it look like? How does it act? Why did it take so long to discover?

....

....

....

....

....

....

....

....

Pick your favorite character in a book or movie and write about what they were like in school. Were they talkative? Shy? Were they good at sports? Explain them in as much detail as possible.

....

....

....

....

....

....

....

....

You find a note in the back of your journal that explains how to use your closet as a time machine. Where do you go first? What do you do? How does traveling in time feel? Do you experience jet lag?

....

....

....

....

....

....

....

....

....

....

....

....

....

....

....

....

....

Look at the front page of the newspaper. Grab phrases or sentences
from any story and combine them to make an original article.

....

....

....

....

....

....

....

....

....

....

....

....

....

....

....

....

....

....

....

You wake up in a foreign country in the house of a native family.
They are extremely friendly but completely different from your family.
Explain what your breakfast that first morning is like.

....

....

....

....

....

....

....

....

Write the story of Cinderella from the point of view of one of the
stepsisters. You think you're a good person. How do you feel about
a new sister joining the family? Are you jealous of her? Do you feel
bad when your mom is mean to her?

....

....

....

....

....

....

....

....

Write an encyclopedia entry about a
fictional town. What kind of food do
the people eat? What language do they
speak? What do they believe in?

Try to write the perfect sentence.
Think about the sounds of the words,
the shapes of the letters, the meaning.

A witch turns your best friend into
a bar of gold, and only you can save
your friend — if only you knew how to
reverse the spell.

On a family trip your little brother
goes missing, and his tracks lead
straight to the middle of a giant tree.
But there's no hole in the tree. Where
could he have gone and how do
you find him?

Write a review of a book or movie that has never been made. Be as positive or as critical as you see fit. Make sure to give a description of what it is about.

....

....

....

....

....

....

....

....

....

....

....

....

....

....

....

....

....

Write a story about a pirate without using visual adjectives. Focus on the smells, the sounds, and the feeling of the boat and the pirate life.

....

....

....

....

....

....

....

....

Write a story through the eyes of an inanimate object (a lightbulb, an umbrella, etc.). What is an average day like? What does it think about? What does it do when it's not being used?

....

....

....

....

....

....

....

....

You are taking a train through a distant land. Write about the landscape you see.

....

....

....

....

....

....

In as much detail as possible, explain what you do from the moment you get up until the time you arrive at school. Try your best not to leave anything out.

....

....

....

....

....

You are about to take a nap by a river, and as you are dozing off, the rush of the river begins to sound like words. What does the river say to you? What does it want you to do?

....

....

....

....

....

You are designing your dream house. What color would the walls be? What special rooms would you have? What music would play inside? Give the reasons behind each decision you make.

....

....

....

....

....

....

....

....

....

....

....

....

....

....

....

....

....

....

Write a letter to your great-great-grandmother. Ask her anything you want to know about your family's history. Tell her about yourself and your family.

....

....

....

....

....

....

....

....

Your parents want you to learn a sport, but you really want to learn the piano instead. Write a letter to your parents convincing them that you'll get the same benefits from piano lessons.

....

....

....

....

....

....

....

....

During a trip to the zoo, your parents walk off to look at the parrots
while you're still looking at the bears. Now that you're alone, one of
the bears turns to you and says, "Get me out of here!" What do you do?

....

....

....

....

....

....

....

....

You learn that you can see the future in a glass of soda. You see
something bad is going to happen to your friend. What is it and what
do you do about it?

....

....

....

....

....

....

....

....

Bandits have taken you into the dark forest. But there's a troll on the other side of the forest who eats bandits for breakfast. How will you lure the bandits there so that the troll can save you?

The letter "k" has mysteriously disappeared from the alphabet. What happened?

You have a ton of homework to do, but your room is full of gnomes.

Your mother tells you to wash the dishes, but when you turn on the faucet, something that isn't water comes out.

It was a fairly dull day, until the planet was invaded.

A girl goes missing at a traveling circus.

You're walking alone down an empty street and fall into a hole. You land in the underground world of Tod, where people speak in rhymes and hate stairs. How do you get back home?

....

....

....

....

....

....

....

....

You have to escape from a castle dungeon and you have only a piece of gum, a slingshot, and a fairy named Pat. How do you get out of the dungeon and avoid the terrible queen?

....

....

....

....

....

....

....

....

If you could live one day without consequences, what would you do?

....

....

....

....

....

....

....

....

....

....

....

....

....

....

....

....

....

....

Where do lost socks go?

What's the best thing about cereal?

You notice that all the clocks
have begun moving too slow.

A boy comes home to find a small package
in the mailbox with no postage stamp,
and it looks as if it's come
a long way.

Write about what happens the day giant fluffy bunnies take over your school.

....

....

....

....

....

....

....

....

Which is better: a pegasus or a unicorn? Make your case.

....

....

....

....

....

....

....

....

What people, recipes, dishes, and decorations always seem to turn up during the holidays? What do you like best about those things? What would you like to replace with something new?

....

....

....

....

....

....

....

....

....

....

....

....

....

....

....

....

....

....

....

Your dog has decided to learn a language. Convince him why French would be a good idea.

....

....

....

....

....

....

Why is everyone walking backward?

....

....

....

....

....

....

Explain to a gold miner from 1849 how e-mail works.

....

....

....

....

....

Describe how it feels to be underwater.

....

....

....

....

....

....

....

....

Write the speech your mom or dad will give at your high school—
graduation party.

....

....

....

....

....

....

....

....

You've just come back from the grocery store and you discover something in the bottom of the bag that you've never seen before and definitely did not buy. What is it, and what do you do with it?

....

....

....

....

....

....

....

....

What is your earliest winter memory?

....

....

....

....

....

....

....

....

If you had to get rid of everything in your closet except for three items, what would you keep? Why?

....

....

....

....

....

....

....

....

....

....

....

....

....

....

....

....

....

....

What is the best thing about spring?

Describe what it's like to run as fast as you can.

If your family had a motto, what would it be?

I am afraid of . . .

It turns out, your next-door neighbor is a leprechaun and you have to prove it to your family.

....

....

....

....

....

....

What does "home for the holidays" mean to you?

....

....

....

....

....

....

If your apartment or house were on fire, what would you save, and why?

....

....

....

....

....

....

What are your family traditions?

....
....
....
....
....
....
....
....

If I didn't care what anyone thought . . .

....
....
....
....
....
....
....
....

I wish I had . . .

....

....

....

....

....

....

....

....

I wish I hadn't . . .

....

....

....

....

....

....

....

....

Rewrite a fairy tale from the point of view of one of the less
important characters.

....

....

....

....

....

....

....

....

....

....

....

....

....

....

....

....

....

....

In the future, everyone
will wear . . .

What are your school lunches like?

Snow

What would you like to be famous for?

Write about something you've lied about.

....

....

....

....

....

....

What do you do after school?

....

....

....

....

....

Describe a flavor of ice cream that reminds you of your favorite place to visit.

....

....

....

....

....

What would it be like to have a mythical creature for a pet? What creature would you choose? What would you do with your pet?

....

....

....

....

....

....

....

....

....

....

....

....

....

....

....

....

....

....

If you could spend a day with your favorite fictional character,
whom would you pick, and what would you do together?

....

....

....

....

....

....

....

....

If you could be famous for just one day, what would you do?

....

....

....

....

....

....

....

If you could trade a sibling for something else, what would it be,
and why? (Or why wouldn't you?)

....

....

....

....

....

....

....

....

....

If you could invent a machine to do one chore for you, what chore
would that be? How would the machine work?

....

....

....

....

....

....

....

....

Choose a character from your favorite video game. They stumble into our "real" world for 24 hours. You are their guide. Describe the day. What would be your highlights? What would they remember the most?

....

....

....

....

....

....

....

....

....

....

....

....

....

....

....

....

Imagine you're an archaeologist searching for a lost treasure. Describe what you see along the way. What are you looking for? Do you find it?

....

....

....

....

....

....

....

....

If you could change one quality about yourself, what would it be? Why?

....

....

....

....

....

....

....

....

....

Lemonade

What would you do if the floor were
actually hot lava?

Write about the life of a
piece of string.

You are a fly on the wall and overhear
a conversation between two famous
people. What are they talking about?

Write five to ten very short updates from your life, from birth until now.

....

....

....

....

....

....

....

....

....

....

....

....

....

....

....

....

....

....

Write about a cookie addict and the intervention their friends
have to try to help.

....

....

....

....

....

....

....

....

Write about a writer having writer's block.

....

....

....

....

....

....

....

....

Write about a tightrope walker who falls.

....

....

....

....

....

....

Write about the worries of a very tall person.

....

....

....

....

....

....

Write from the perspective of a tree turned into lumber.

....

....

....

....

....

....

Write about a game of truth or dare gone wrong.

Write about a lion hunting its prey.

Write about a kitten having a nightmare and its mother comforting it.

Write about a human who has turned into a dolphin.

Write from the perspective of a baby who doesn't want to take a nap.

Write about a rebellious teenager in detention.

....

....

....

....

....

....

....

....

Write about an escape from jail.

....

....

....

....

....

....

....

....

Write about the world's oldest person.

....

....

....

....

....

....

....

....

....

Write about a girl's babysitting experience.

....

....

....

....

....

....

....

....

Write about a little girl begging for a pony.

....

....

....

....

....

....

Write about an ice cube abandoned under the fridge.

....

....

....

....

....

....

Write from a balloon's perspective after being released into the air.

....

....

....

....

....

....

Write about a person obsessed with the color yellow.

You have hair down to your feet, and it is also the source of your secret superpowers. What are they?

....

....

....

....

....

....

....

....

....

....

....

....

....

....

....

....

....

....

Write about a kid who is about to do a dare she really doesn't want to do.

....

....

....

....

....

....

Write about 15 people trapped in a cave during a tornado.

....

....

....

....

....

....

Write from the donkey's perspective during a game of pin the tail on the donkey.

....

....

....

....

....

....

Invent a new dance move.

What's the funniest thing about someone you love?

Write from a cow's perspective while it is being milked.

Describe the taste and texture of your favorite (or least favorite) kind of food you eat with a spoon.

Your feet are really smelly, but you have no sense of smell, so when someone asks, you blame anything and everything around you for the foul odor. Go.

....

....

....

....

....

....

....

....

Write about a game of hide-and-seek that has gotten out of hand.

....

....

....

....

....

....

....

....

You've traveled to a distant planet covered in something soft and squishy that is hard to identify. What methods do you use to identify the material this planet is made up of? What are the inhabitants of this planet like?

....

....

....

....

....

....

....

....

Invent a new handshake and write instructions for how to do it, who can use it, and when it is used.

....

....

....

....

....

....

....

....

Make up a new language and share the most commonly used phrases for travelers who encounter speakers of this new language.

You're a mother who's on her way to pick up her daughter from the principal's office.

....

....

....

....

....

....

Describe the first time you went to school.

....

....

....

....

....

....

If you had to do the thing you were most afraid of, what would it be?

....

....

....

....

....

....

What if you had the power to grant wishes to other people? How would you decide whom to help and when?

What story from television or books would you most like to enter? What character would you play?

You have been transported inside your computer. How do you get out?

You are going to a desert island where you will spend the rest of your days, and you can bring only one book. Which one will you choose? Why?

Create a magazine about being a kid. What would it be called?
What topics would you cover?

....

....

....

....

....

....

....

....

....

....

....

....

....

....

....

....

....

....

....

Describe the youngest person you know, and list their daily
activities.

....

....

....

....

....

....

....

....

Tell us about the oldest person you know, and describe their
day-to-day life.

....

....

....

....

....

....

....

....

Describe your favorite relative. What do they look and sound like?
What are their best qualities?

....

....

....

....

....

....

Describe your dream tree house.

....

....

....

....

....

....

Pick an inanimate object on your desk (a lamp, a pencil,
an eraser, etc.) and write a thank-you note to it.

....

....

....

....

....

....

Interview your best friend and record their answers to all your questions.

....

....

....

....

....

....

....

....

....

....

....

....

....

....

....

....

....

You are from Jupiter and visiting Earth. Report back to your home planet
about a trip to a supermarket on Earth. Use as much detail as possible,
and remember: everything is completely new and bizarre to you.

....

....

....

....

....

....

....

....

....

....

....

....

....

....

....

....

....

....

The government is about to pass a law outlawing candy. Write a letter explaining why all kids have the right to eat sweets.

....

....

....

....

....

....

....

....

A mad scientist offers to create an animal for you to have as a pet. Combine the traits of at least four animals to craft the perfect pet, explaining the advantage of each characteristic.

....

....

....

....

....

....

....

....

What is something that you wish someone had told you about being a kid?

Imagine that every smartphone on earth sprouted arms and legs and ran away. Would they be friendly? Would they form their own society?

Write a poem about a bird that is afraid of heights.

What do you do for fun?

Think of a moment when you were humiliated. Write about the feelings, the smells, the sounds, and the experience without explaining the cause of your embarrassment. Use as much detail as possible.

....

....

....

....

....

....

....

....

....

....

....

....

....

....

....

....

....

....

....

Write a story about a clown who loses his sense of humor.
What makes him lose it? What must he do to get it back?

....

....

....

....

....

....

....

....

Write a review of your dream concert. Which bands play? Which songs
do they play? At what venue? Do they crowd-surf?

....

....

....

....

....

....

....

....

You are eating dinner at your grandma's house, when suddenly, the food on your plate comes to life. Only you notice. What do you do?

....

....

....

....

....

You are setting off on a journey to slay a dragon and can bring one character from a book or film with you. Whom do you bring? Write the dialogue between you and the character.

....

....

....

....

....

Write a story from the point of view of a raccoon. What is the city like at night? Why do you knock over trash cans? Do you get along with the other raccoons?

....

....

....

....

....

You are going to start a food truck but need a plan first. Write out your business strategy. What kind of food will you serve? What will your truck look like? What will be on your menu? What will be your food truck's name?

....

....

....

....

....

....

....

....

....

....

....

....

....

....

....

....

....

You are a vegetarian tiger.

You come to school one Monday and find that a robot is leading your class instead of your teacher.

If you could talk to your parents when they were your age, what would you say?

What is the best meal of the day?

You are putting together a crew to sail around the world. You're the captain and need a first mate (your right-hand), a boatswain (to make sure jobs on the ship get done), a gunner (running the guns on the boat), a carpenter (to do repairs on board), a cook (to make the food), and a musician (to lead sea shanties). Write your choice for each position (either people you know, fictional characters, or celebrities) as well as a brief explanation of why each is the right choice for the job.

....

....

....

....

....

....

Write a poem that uses as many words that begin with the first letter of your name as possible.

....

....

....

....

....

....

....

....

You are digging a hole in your backyard and find an ancient book.
You clean off the cover and open to the first page.

....

....

....

....

....

....

Write a poem about your favorite song. Try to capture more than
just the lyrics; focus on the sounds, the way it affects you,
and the energy of the music.

....

....

....

....

....

....

Imagine that your favorite actor, athlete, or musician worked in a
completely different profession. Write a day in their alternate life.

....

....

....

....

....

....

Write a ghost story. Focus on pacing and dramatic timing to build as much tension as you can. Read the story aloud as you write to make sure it will be scary to hear on a dark and stormy night!

....

....

....

....

....

....

....

....

....

....

....

....

....

....

....

....

....

Set a stopwatch for five minutes. Start the timer and then write down every single thing that comes to mind until the time runs out. Try your best to turn off your filter and put every thought you have onto paper.

....

....

....

....

....

....

....

....

....

....

....

....

....

....

....

....

....

You must try to sell a disgusting vegetable. Write a television commercial to get people excited to try it. Make sure to write both the dialogue that the viewer will hear and the action that the viewer will see.

....

....

....

....

....

....

....

....

You are a superhero's little brother or sister. You are just an average kid, but your older sibling can lift cars, fly, and break through brick walls. Write a diary entry about the day you learn of your sibling's superpowers. Are you excited? Nervous? Jealous?

....

....

....

....

....

....

....

....

Write the story of how you got your name. Either interview your parents to find the true story or write an imaginary story.

....

....

....

....

....

....

You are walking through an alleyway and find a pair of ancient eyeglasses. You clean them and try them on, and suddenly you can see back in time. What do you see?

....

....

....

....

....

....

Imagine that you are one of your grandparents. Write a journal entry in their voice. What did you do today? What did you think about? What is important to you?

....

....

....

....

....

Write about a character from a song.

Your dog has won a free trip to the moon. What do you pack for him?

Write a newspaper ad to sell anything you want.

There is a sea monster in your bedroom. Why?

If your favorite toy could talk and walk, what would you talk about together? What would you do together?

....

....

....

....

....

....

....

....

Think back on a conversation that was very important to you and write it out as a scene in a story. Besides including what each person says, make sure to use details to describe the setting, the tone of the dialogue, and the reaction of each character.

....

....

....

....

....

....

....

....

Imagine that you are the first explorer to discover your hometown and its current inhabitants. Write a report about the lay of the land, the people's habits, and the dangers of this new place.

....

....

....

....

....

....

....

....

Write an article about a sporting event, either one you played in or one you watched. Try to make it as much like a newspaper article as possible. What are the important events? Who would be interviewed? What background information is needed?

....

....

....

....

....

....

....

....

Think up a plot for a movie. Write a one-page summary that you could pitch to a producer. Make sure to tell about the characters, the setting, and the story, but leave the ending out of the pitch to keep the producer wanting more.

....

....

....

....

....

....

....

....

....

....

....

....

....

....

....

....

....

....

If you could talk for an unlimited time to anyone in the world,
who would it be, and what would you talk about?

....

....

....

....

....

A witch transforms you into a talking cookie. What do
you do to get your human form back?

....

....

....

....

....

....

Mrs. Tinn is an old woman living in a large mansion with 14
rabbits. Every morning she bakes 20 pies. These pies have
magical properties . . .

....

....

....

....

....

If you could eat only one thing your whole life, what would it be?

You get to spend a whole day with your favorite band/singer. Describe what you all do together.

You are the director of a new animated film. What is the film about?

While poking around the garden with your friend, you uncover a hidden pond. Inside the water you see four frogs. On each of their backs there is a letter.
What do the frogs need you to do for them?

Write a story with the title "How Ladybugs Got Their Dots."

....

....

....

....

....

....

....

....

....

....

....

....

....

....

....

....

....

Write about two hamsters that decide to go on a journey to the center of the Earth.

....

....

....

....

....

....

You become the king/queen of the world. What things do you change to make the world a better place?

....

....

....

....

....

....

The doughnut apocalypse is coming soon. What do you do to get ready?

....

....

....

....

....

....

A mad scientist has an evil plan to conquer the world.
You are the only one who can stop him.

....

....

....

....

....

....

....

....

Two villains start robbing a house, but are stopped by a scary sound and
flee the scene. The sound turns out to be the pet parrot, making noises.
Tell this story.

....

....

....

....

....

....

....

....

Take out every toy you own and set them up in your room. Now, write a story of how they all wound up there and what they're doing. Remember to account for the variety of characters.

....

....

....

....

....

....

....

....

....

....

....

....

....

....

....

....

....

You are lying in a hammock under a shady tree. A bird drops a rolled-up
piece of paper in your lap containing 20 words. What is the message?

....

....

....

....

....

Imagine you open your own restaurant. Give it a name.
What kind of food is served?

....

....

....

....

....

....

Three talking purple goats are having a picnic in front of your house. They
ask you to help them plan some activities since they're new to the area.

....

....

....

....

....

....

Instead of a golden lamp, you find a cheap silver-colored flashlight. When you press the button, a small genie appears. "You get three wishes that undo things. What will you undo?" he asks.

....

....

....

....

....

....

....

....

At a party, you take a sip of the orange-colored punch. It tickles your tongue, and for the rest of the day you cannot speak any lies or half-truths. How does this day go?

....

....

....

....

....

....

....

....

One day, the smallest creature in the world decided to try extra-hard to become the biggest, and it worked! How did it happen?

Describe the setting of a different universe, where ice is hot and flowers are prickly.

Write a poem about somebody who is half human and half house.

What is the name of a person who has feet that are six times too big?

For you, water is poison! Write about what life is like, avoiding water.

....

....

....

....

....

....

....

....

....

....

....

....

....

....

....

....

....

....

One day, all your gummy bears and gummy worms come alive! They look at you expectantly. You can't eat them now. Write about your adventures together.

....

....

....

....

....

....

....

....

....

....

....

....

....

....

....

....

....

....

Go to a bookshelf and pick out a book that has a red spine. Flip to page 42.
What's the first word? That's your first word, too. Go!

....

....

....

....

....

....

....

....

....

Scientists discovered a new planet that may hold life-forms, and they require
a kid to take the helm of the spaceship because it's a really small ship,
and because the journey could take a lifetime. You apply for the job and
are accepted.

....

....

....

....

....

....

....

....

You drop a tomato and some cheese in your backyard, and where they landed
a pizza tree sprouts. What happens next?

....

....

....

....

....

....

You have a pet chicken named Edgar. Write about Edgar's day-to-day life.

....

....

....

....

....

....

You were born with a strange ability. You can crack open coconuts, oranges,
watermelons, and other round fruit using just your mind. What's a day in
your life like?

....

....

....

....

....

....

Instead of hair, you have pasta.

You are surrounded by hot lava!
What happens next?

If you could be anyone for a day,
who would you be? Why?

Track the path of the next bug you meet.
What is it up to? Where is it going?
What do you think it is thinking about?

One day you buy a necklace that you discover makes
you fluent in any language. What happens next?

....

....

....

....

....

....

....

....

Make up a new game involving pocket lint, pennies,
and a mystery object of your choosing.

....

....

....

....

....

....

....

....

Invent a new form of communication. Describe its major features and whether this is an improvement or not over our current methods of communicating.

....

....

....

....

....

....

....

....

You have a car that can drive in the air. Write about your (mis)adventures.

....

....

....

....

....

....

....

....

Invent a new holiday and describe the rituals and festivities that are
celebrated on that day.

....

....

....

....

....

....

....

....

....

....

....

....

....

....

....

....

....

....

Make up a new identity, or alias, for yourself. What is your new name?
How do you dress now? What types of things do you enjoy doing?

....

....

....

....

....

....

....

....

....

....

....

....

....

....

....

....

....

Write about a time in your life when you had to be brave. What situation were you in? How did you find that strength?

....

....

....

....

....

....

....

....

Tell us about the person you admire most. Why do you admire him or her? Would you like to be like this person?

....

....

....

....

....

....

....

....

One day you find a Tyrannosaurus rex sitting on the sidewalk with his big
head in his small hands, crying. What do you do next?

....

....

....

....

....

....

If you could invent a new form of transportation — one the world has never
seen — what would it be?

....

....

....

....

....

....

Pretend you have a pet pig and describe an adventure you go on together.

....

....

....

....

....

....

Give yourself a compliment, a really
long, over-the-top, verging-on-too-much
compliment.

If you could develop a new skill
instantly, what would it be?

Describe a daily routine.

If you could travel anywhere
under the sea, where would you go?

Write a letter to an imaginary pen pal in another country. Where is your pen pal from? What do you want to know about your pen pal's life?

....

....

....

....

....

....

....

....

....

....

....

....

....

....

....

....

....

The Milky Way is only one of many galaxies in the universe. Name another
galaxy (real or imaginary) and describe the planets that exist in this
galaxy and the climates of each of them.

....

....

....

....

....

....

....

....

....

....

....

....

....

....

....

....

....

The people of Ice Cream Island are desperately in need of new ice cream flavors. Please invent one (or more!) for them.

....

....

....

....

....

....

....

....

Invent a world where everything is upside down. How do people manage? Can they even drink out of glasses?

....

....

....

....

....

....

....

....

Describe a time when someone surprised you in a good way.
What was the occasion?

....

....

....

....

....

....

If you could do anything you want, but you had to do it all the time,
what would it be?

....

....

....

....

....

....

What inventions do you think we should come up with next?

....

....

....

....

....

....

What do you wish more people thought about?

What do babies dream about?

What are your favorite things to do during summer?

What is the most valuable thing you own?

If you could be any kind of junk food, which would you be, and why?
Who would your junk food friends be? How would you defend yourself
from being eaten by hungry humans?

....

....

....

....

....

....

....

....

....

....

....

....

....

....

....

....

....

Create a new way of making friends. Would it be easy or hard?
Would other people like to do it, or would it be your secret method?

....

....

....

....

....

....

....

....

If you were to build a time capsule of all of your favorite things,
what would you put in it, and why?

....

....

....

....

....

....

....

....

If you could mind read, what do you think you would learn about other people?

....

....

....

....

....

....

....

....

Close your eyes.

....

....

....

....

....

....

....

....

On your first day of preschool, you study really hard and end up graduating high school by the afternoon. What do you do with the remainder of your childhood years?

....

....

....

....

....

....

....

....

....

....

....

....

....

....

....

....

If you could build something for your family or friends,
what would you build?

....

....

....

....

....

....

Describe your absolute least favorite thing to do.
Why is it so terrible?

....

....

....

....

....

....

What do you think is the coolest job you could possibly have?

....

....

....

....

....

....

You win a huge amount of money, but you must not spend the money on yourself. How do you spend the money?

....

....

....

....

....

....

....

....

....

....

....

....

....

....

....

....

....

....

What are you carrying in your
bag right now?

What do you do when you don't
want to do your homework?

If you could be any fictional character,
who would you be?

If you could bring one kind of
dinosaur back to life, which kind
would it be?

What do you think you'll be like when you're grown up?

....

....

....

....

....

....

....

....

....

You carve an elephant out of soap and leave it in the kitchen overnight.
When you return for it in the morning, it is gone, and there is a trail
of broken peanut shells leading out the front door.

....

....

....

....

....

....

....

....

Write a story that ends with the line "He had neither arms nor legs, but he had a lot of bravery."

You and a friend find a rocket ship.

....

....

....

....

....

....

Write a haiku about your shoes (remember: a haiku is a poem
of three lines; the first line has five syllables, the second
has seven, and the last has five).

....

....

....

....

....

....

You find an injured baby owl, take it home with you, and
discover it can talk. What do you say to each other?

....

....

....

....

....

Write a love letter to your favorite food.

....

....

....

....

....

....

....

....

Today is going to be the best day of your life. What happens
from the moment you get out of bed to the moment you go back
to sleep at night?

....

....

....

....

....

....

....

....

It's only a little money.

Let's go to the park.

That was broken before
I was even born!

You left what, where?

Write about a day in the life of an old, used prom dress.

What would a school look like if you designed it from scratch? What
kind of classes would be offered? What would never happen? What would
the teachers be like? What would the principal be like? What kind of
building would this school be in?

Have you asked your parents about their childhood? Write a story about them when they were your age. Here are some questions to get you started with your interviews:

....

What did you like to eat?

....

....

....

....

What was the best dish your mom would make for you?

....

....

....

....

What did you want to be when you grew up?

....

....

....

....

What is your funniest memory?

....

....

....

....

....

....

....

....

Who were your closest friends?
....

....

....

What did you like to do with them?
....

....

....

Tell me about a time you were naughty.
....

....

....

....

....

....

....

....

....

Pretend you're a tiny fish. Convince a hungry shark not to eat you.

....

....

....

....

....

....

....

....

There's a man who lives in a tree. You've never seen him because he's hidden by the leaves. One day, a ladder comes down with a note asking you to join him for lunch. What happens?

....

....

....

....

....

....

....

....

Did you know that when you write thank-you notes you are likely to get more gifts and kindness? Think of something someone has given you or done for you. On this page, write a nice note to the person.

....

....

....

....

....

....

....

....

....

....

....

....

....

....

....

....

....

....

What would happen if you wore a Japanese wrestling mask every day to
school — and no one noticed, except the science teacher, who was wearing
a Mexican wrestling mask?

....

....

....

....

....

You're out shopping with your mom or dad. In one of the stores, the
merchandise begins talking. The items are planning a rebellion and
need your help. What kind of store is it, and what happens next?

....

....

....

....

....

You're the only one home, when the doorbell rings. You open the door,
and there are three badgers dressed in Girl Scout uniforms. They're
trying to sell you cookies, but you know it's a trick.

....

....

....

....

....

If you could be any vegetable,
what would you be?

Just try it.

You'll catch your death!

I'm on my way!

For your birthday, your uncle gives you a large empty box with instructions. Once you climb in and close the lid, you will be transported wherever you want but with one condition: you may return home only if you bring back a creature that is native to that other land.

....

....

....

....

....

....

....

....

....

....

....

....

....

....

....

....

....

One day you realize all your senses are switched: you can smell sounds, hear textures, taste colors, etc. Describe the world around you.

....

....

....

....

....

....

....

....

....

....

....

....

....

....

....

....

....

....

Pick a character from a book and write the "About Me" they would put on their website. If you're on a roll: What are this character's favorite books? Favorite movies? Favorite quotes (make them up!)?

....

....

....

....

....

....

....

....

Write the scariest short story you could tell around a campfire.

....

....

....

....

....

....

....

....

Nice outfit.

....

....

....

....

....

Late one night, you discover an abandoned UFO in the
middle of a field outside an abandoned farmhouse.

....

....

....

....

....

You're trapped in a fortune cookie factory, held
against your will. What do you write on the fortunes
in an attempt to save yourself?

....

....

....

....

....

Write a poem that would make your teacher laugh.

Write a to-do list that a famous villain would use.

Imagine a conversation between one of your friends and a historical figure.

Write a conversation from the perspective of your silverware.

Write about a holiday from the perspective of the family pet.

....

....

....

....

....

....

....

....

....

....

....

....

....

....

....

....

....

....

Write about a fancy dinner from the perspective of the cranberries.

....

....

....

....

....

....

....

....

....

Write a postcard from one fairy tale character to another.

....

....

....

....

....

....

....

....

....

Describe an alien's bedroom. Do they even have bedrooms?

....

....

....

....

....

....

....

....

Write a story using the following words: chandelier, pig, hubbub.

....

....

....

....

....

....

....

....

Open a magazine at random, and find the first picture of a person you can. Now open it again, and find a picture of a place. Write about what would happen if that person were in that place.

....

....

....

....

....

....

....

....

....

....

....

....

....

....

....

....

....

....

Imagine what's below the streets of a faraway city you've never been to.

....

....

....

....

....

Write about your earliest memory.

....

....

....

....

....

Write about the worst thing you've ever eaten.

....

....

....

....

....

Write about a character who everyone thinks is evil, but who
is actually just on a quest for the perfect sandwich.

....

....

....

....

....

....

....

....

Describe the perfect sandwich.

....

....

....

....

....

....

....

....

You are a baby. Persuade someone
to burp you.

There is a giraffe tied to your
kitchen table. Why?

Write about a moose that moves
into a small apartment.

Write about a person who moves
into a giant's mailbox.

Write about a walk or a trip you take almost every day — from your
house to school, for example — as if it's in a guidebook to your city.
What do you hope people will notice or look out for?

....

....

....

....

....

....

....

....

....

....

....

....

....

....

....

....

....

....

Write about the most fun recess you've ever had.

....

....

....

....

....

....

....

....

Write down everything you know about one of your family members.

....

....

....

....

....

....

....

....

Think of a picture you've seen of yourself as a baby. Write what you imagine you were thinking when that picture was taken.

....

....

....

....

....

....

Write about a family of tiny people who build dollhouses.

....

....

....

....

....

....

Write about a family of giants who are just trying to find a good place to play ball.

....

....

....

....

....

....

Write a series of interview questions you would ask a person who lives
2,000 years in the future. Then answer them.

....

....

....

....

....

....

....

....

....

....

....

....

....

....

....

....

....

....

Write about a conversation your cereal would have with itself while floating in a bowl of milk.

Two trees are yelling at each other.

Write a poem in which every line ends with a question mark.

You've been assigned the task of inventing the world's greatest pizza — what ingredients will you choose?

Copy one of the things you've written in this book here,
but change the punctuation so that its meaning changes.

....

....

....

....

....

....

....

....

Write down everything you don't know about your neighbors.

....

....

....

....

....

....

....

....

Write a letter to your first teacher. Then imagine what
your teacher would write back.

....

....

....

....

....

....

....

....

....

....

....

....

....

....

....

....

....

....

Write a poem in which every line ends with a food.

....

....

....

....

....

....

....

....

....

....

....

....

....

....

....

....

....

....

Write down everything you remember happening when you were five years old.

....

....

....

....

....

....

....

....

Describe what you see when you look out your bedroom window
(at 7:00 a.m., noon, 6:00 p.m., and at midnight).

....

....

....

....

....

....

....

....

A couple of cars next to each other at a stoplight are having a conversation.

....

....

....

....

....

....

Write a story about a hedgehog and a warthog that live in a playground.

....

....

....

....

....

There's been a mistake. Two children think that you are a witch,
and they've begun eating the gingerbread house you live in.

....

....

....

....

....

You suddenly find yourself on the other side of your mirror. How did you get there? What's it like? Will you stay? How will you get back?

....

....

....

....

....

....

....

....

....

....

....

....

....

....

....

....

....

....

What do you do when you don't
have to do anything?

If you had to tell someone something
they wouldn't want to hear,
how would you do it?

Describe what your breath smells like
when you don't brush your teeth.

What do you do on a Saturday?

Write a story about a friendship between a whale and a
snail. Be sure to name them!

....

....

....

....

....

....

....

....

You find a tree that grows dreams. What dreams will you
pick from the tree?

....

....

....

....

....

....

....

....

Write a story about a girl named Maria and the mouse
who lives in her pocket.

....

....

....

....

....

....

....

....

Imagine you wake up one morning to find you are very tiny. Write about
your day — don't worry, you'll be back to your normal size tomorrow.

....

....

....

....

....

....

....

....

What makes you different from anyone else, and why?

....

....

....

....

....

....

Do you think you are more like your mother or your father
or another relative? Why? How?

....

....

....

....

....

....

Describe what being a good friend means to you.

....

....

....

....

....

....

Describe yourself in ten symbols. What do they mean?

....

....

....

....

....

....

....

....

....

....

....

....

....

....

....

....

....

....

Write about a time you helped someone without them knowing.

Where were you born? Using your imagination, describe the day you were born.

What makes you sad?

What do you do to cheer people up?

If your life were a movie, how would you like it to play out?

....

....

....

....

....

....

....

....

Use five words to describe yourself. Then make sentences that aren't about
you, using each of the words. Turn the sentences into a story.

....

....

....

....

....

....

....

....

Pick a color, a smell, and a place. Pick a person, a thing, and an animal. Now create a story using all your choices.

....

....

....

....

....

....

....

....

....

....

....

....

....

....

....

....

....

....

Write about someone you care about in five sentences. Think about why they are important to you and what makes them special. Why should people get to know them?

....

....

....

....

....

....

....

....

Write a newspaper article. The headline is "New House to Be Built at Manor Lake."

....

....

....

....

....

....

....

....

Describe a recent encounter with an animal that was not a cat or a dog.

....

....

....

....

....

....

....

....

Write a story that starts with "The earthquake swallowed my house, and we were falling for hours."

....

....

....

....

....

....

....

....

Invent a story about how the world began.

....

....

....

....

....

....

....

....

....

....

....

....

....

....

....

....

....

....

If you had a dream bicycle, what would it be like? Describe all its features and how people would react to it.

....

....

....

....

....

....

....

....

A government agent wants to know all about where you live and what your life is like. How much do you tell her?

....

....

....

....

....

....

....

....

Write out your name, and think of one adjective that describes you for each letter of your name.

What is the most important smell?

Describe a sound you hear every day.

Imagine a sound that is the most wonderful *and* the most terrible sound.

You get to have any kind of parade you choose. Write about the floats, the people, and the crowds.

....

....

....

....

....

....

....

....

....

....

....

....

....

....

....

....

....

....

A very tall man in a long black coat and dark sunglasses offers you one wish, but it has to benefit the entire country. What's the wish you make, and how does it help?

....

....

....

....

....

....

....

....

Write a story titled "The Dog Who Couldn't Bark."

....

....

....

....

....

....

....

....

You get to have a personal servant, but you can only choose from a selection of monsters. Do you want the mummy? The werewolf? The Loch Ness monster? What are the benefits and drawbacks of your monster?

....

....

....

....

....

....

....

....

....

You're sitting at a table in the back of a pizza restaurant, when you feel something moving around your knees. You lift up the edge of the tablecloth to see a small animal that looks at you. In a raspy voice, it whispers, "Hide me!"

....

....

....

....

....

....

....

....

Write a story about a snake that dreams of becoming
a professional basketball player.

....

....

....

....

....

....

A shoe company is releasing a brand-new type of shoe,
and they want your advice.

....

....

....

....

....

....

You're a food critic. Write a review of a restaurant.
Use all five senses!

....

....

....

....

....

....

If you could control plants, what would you do with that power?

What does the word "hope" mean to you?

You set up a lemonade stand, and five minutes later your neighbors set one up, too. What do you do?

Write a joke about kangaroos.

Write a review of a movie you have recently seen. Don't spoil the ending, but give plot details and your opinion so the readers can decide if they want to see it.

....

....

....

....

....

....

....

....

....

....

....

....

....

....

....

....

....

....

You are a world traveler. Write a journal entry from one of the
destinations you have visited and what adventures you had there.

....

....

....

....

....

....

....

....

....

....

....

....

....

....

....

....

....

....

Write a story titled "The Pirate Who Smiled Too Much."

....

....

....

....

....

....

....

....

Write a confused conversation between a bus driver and a
tourist trying to get to a famous attraction.

....

....

....

....

....

....

....

....

Imagine someone you know has been put under a sleeping spell. Now is your only chance to tell them how you feel without consequences. Would you tell them a secret? Would you tell them a story?

....

....

....

....

....

....

....

....

You are an underwater explorer and you find an entire civilization on the seafloor. What does it look like? What creatures live there? What is the language and community like?

....

....

....

....

....

....

....

....

You have the opportunity to get into a time machine and travel back to any time. The catch is that you have to stay wherever you end up, and must pick a time before you were born. Which year do you choose? Describe your new life.

....

....

....

....

....

....

....

....

....

....

....

....

....

....

....

....

....

Oh no, you're stuck inside of a video game! How do you
beat the levels and escape?

....

....

....

....

....

....

....

....

You're the principal of your school. You are leading a
parent meeting and proposing some changes. What changes
would you make and why?

....

....

....

....

....

....

....

....

You are a giraffe, going about your regular giraffe life, but one day you eat a loaf and you can suddenly speak human languages. What would you say to the first person you saw?

A fork has been following you. Why?

Your classmate steals your lunch one day. What do you do?

Write about a time when you were scared.

It's topsy-turvy day, and all the rules are backward.
Write about what you do that day.

....

....

....

....

....

....

....

....

....

....

....

....

....

....

....

....

....

....

You are given the power to transform into any person or animal. Whichever
one you choose, you must stay in that form for the rest of your life. What
do you choose, and what's your life like?

....

....

....

....

....

....

....

....

....

....

....

....

....

....

....

....

....

....

You are applying for your dream job. Write about your qualifications
and why you would be a great candidate to hire.

....

....

....

....

....

You are walking down the street and have to choose one person to
give just a little money to. It can be anyone. Whom do you choose
and why? How do they react?

....

....

....

....

....

....

Write a poem about a stranger.

....

....

....

....

....

....

You were just hired by someone important to write a speech for them.
What do you want them to say?

....

....

....

....

....

....

....

....

You get to choose to be any color in the universe: blue, orange, purple,
or anything else. Choose your color and say why you chose it.

....

....

....

....

....

....

....

....

You are Otka, hermit crab and
king of your fish tank.
How do you rule your kingdom?

You are a farmer and you've created
a hybrid plant that will change
the world. What is it?

Write the thoughts your pet or
a friend's pet has every day.

What was the strangest thing
you saw this week?

Invent the most disgusting dish you can think of, and write the recipe,
with exact measurements and instructions.

....

....

....

....

....

....

....

....

....

....

....

....

....

....

....

....

....

....

....

A famous singer approaches you because he wants you to write
a song for him called "It's Way Too Loud." Write the lyrics.

....

....

....

....

....

....

....

....

Pick any two animals and imagine what they would look like if they were
combined into one animal. Write about a day in that new animal's life.

....

....

....

....

....

....

....

....

Look at yourself in a mirror for ten minutes and write all your sights and thoughts down.

Choose a painting, and then make up a story about the scene taking place in it.

Write about your favorite historical era.

···

···

···

···

···

···

···

···

···

···

···

···

···

···

···

···

···

···

Choose a lyric from your favorite song and write a story based on it.

....

....

....

....

....

....

Describe how you get ready for bed.

....

....

....

....

....

Describe your favorite hidden spot.

....

....

....

....

....

List the food you ate today then write a list of the colors in those foods.
Use the colors of those foods in a story.

Write about a time you had trouble
with some food.

Write about the first time you heard
your favorite song.

Write about a crow waiting
at a bus stop.

Puffer fish puff up when they're
scared or mad. Write what you would
say to a puffer fish to get
him all puffy.

Write about a "first."

....

....

....

....

....

....

Write about a late-night drive.

....

....

....

....

....

....

Write a letter to a gopher.

....

....

....

....

....

Trace the length of each line of an already-written poem and write your own poem using those line lengths.

....

....

....

....

....

....

....

....

Write a speech convincing your classmates to elect you class president.

....

....

....

....

....

....

....

....

....

Hyperbole is when you make a huge exaggeration, like "my friends are a million times better than yours." Write five hyperbolic sentences, then write a story using hyperbole.

....

....

....

....

....

....

....

....

....

....

....

....

....

....

....

....

....

....

Alliteration is when words near each other repeat the same consonant sound. For example "Llamas like to collaborate with leopards." Write a poem full of alliteration.

....

....

....

....

....

....

....

....

....

....

....

....

....

....

....

....

....

....

Who is the funniest person you know?
What makes that person so funny?

Your hair catches on fire.

If you could smell only one smell
for the rest of your life, what
would that smell be?

Your friend gives you a scarf of
invisibility. What do you
use it for?

You meet an alien from outer space. What are the first
five things you explain about Earth?

....

....

....

....

....

....

Write a poem about a friend.

....

....

....

....

....

....

Write a short story, and make one of your characters
sing a song that you love.

....

....

....

....

....

....

If you could invent a sport, what would it be,
and what would the rules be?

....

....

....

....

....

....

....

....

....

....

....

....

....

....

....

....

....

....

Write a play where you get to be an adult and
all the adults in your life are kids.

....

....

....

....

....

....

....

....

....

....

....

....

....

....

....

....

....

....

....

If you were asked to be in charge of the world for a day,
what kinds of changes would you make?

....

....

....

....

....

....

....

....

....

What kinds of things would you do with an extra arm?
What about an extra leg?

....

....

....

....

....

....

....

....

You step through a doorway that sends you back in time to the Stone Age.
What is the Stone Age like? Whom do you meet? What do you do?

....

....

....

....

....

....

....

....

....

....

....

....

....

....

....

....

....

....

What if you had a magical bag that would compress anything you put
inside it into a carryable weight and size? What would you take with
you everywhere you went? What would this bag look like?

....

....

....

....

....

....

....

....

Your grandpa just told you a family secret. What is it?

....

....

....

....

....

....

....

....

Write a story from the point of view of the smallest fish in the sea. Are you always nervous about being eaten? How do you assert your individuality in your school of fish?

....

....

....

....

....

....

....

....

....

....

....

....

....

....

....

....

....

Imagine you're a book reviewer, reading the writing in this book.
Write some reviews of your writing.

....

....

....

....

....

....

....

....

....

....

....

....

....

....

....

....

....

....

Interview yourself. Interview your interviewer self, too.

You get to be half human, half animal — choose your animal
and describe your new strengths.

....

....

....

....

....

....

Write a poem that describes your last trip to the dentist.

....

....

....

....

....

....

You run into a werewolf while you're on a stroll through
the local cemetery. He looks hungry.

....

....

....

....

....

A head of lettuce tells you that there are also lettuce legs, lettuce arms, and lettuce bodies back at the farm. You have to help these lettuce heads get their bodies back!

The pirate life is glorified in books and movies. You are a real pirate who wants the world to know that your life is not so easy. Write a letter to a newspaper explaining the hardships of the sea. Make sure to use the pirate voice and language throughout your letter.

....

....

....

....

....

....

....

....

....

....

....

....

....

....

....

....

....

Invent a new kind of burrito. What goes in it and what is it wrapped with?

Suddenly you're a huge celebrity. What's the first thing you do?

You discover you have a long-lost twin. What do you want to talk to them about?

In your cereal box, you expect to find cereal, but instead you find a tiny puppy who has eaten all the cereal in the box.

You see a really sad-looking mermaid on a rock by the water. What do you do to cheer her up?

Write a story that begins at the end and works backward. Think of ways to use this to your advantage. How does it change what the reader knows and wants to know next?

....

....

....

....

....

....

....

....

....

....

....

....

....

....

....

....

....

....

....

Describe the time when you laughed the hardest.

....

....

....

....

....

....

Rice, mashed potatoes, yogurt, and ice cream.

....

....

....

....

....

Do dogs go to heaven?

....

....

....

....

....

About the author: Now that you have written a book, write your
biography. Here are some details to include: Where were you raised?
What are your passions?

Advance praise: The stories, poems, and other writing you did in this book will be published. Write some reviews that will go on the back of your book to entice people to pick it up and read it.